UNION BLISS WEDDING PLANNER

UNION ♥ BLISS WEDDING PLANNER

YOUR ULTIMATE GUIDE TO A PERFECT DAY

First Edition

Claudia Frost

Book Cover design by Claudia Frost
Cover Image by Natali Mias / stock.adobe.com
Cover copyright © 2024 by Claudia Frost

First Edition: 2024

ISBN: 9798878648462

www.unionblisss.co.za
Email: info@unionbliss.co.za

Table of Contents

HOW TO USE THIS PLANNER?
GETTING STARTED
   SHOULD WE INVITE THEM?
   IS A WEDDING PLANNER RIGHT FOR YOU?
THE NEXT STEP
   ASSEMBLING YOUR I-DO CREW:
SECURING THE DREAM
NOT LONG NOW
JUST AROUND THE CORNER
THE FINAL COUNTDOWN
MOMENTS BEFORE FOREVER
IT HAS ALL BEEN WORTH IT!
   THE UNOFFICIAL, YET ABSOLUTELY ESSENTIAL WEDDING
   DAY ITINERARY
NAVIGATING POST-WEDDING BLISS
STRESS MANAGEMENT
SETTING THE BUDGET
WEDDING BUDGET
WEDDING PURCHASES
VENDORS
GUEST LIST
   YOUR WEDDING VIP ROSTER
THE FINAL STROKE OF YOUR WEDDING MASTERPIECE
GET IN TOUCH

How to use this planner?

Dive into the exhilarating universe of wedding planning, a realm teeming with delightful quirks and unexpected challenges at every turn. Imagine embarking on a thrilling escapade, akin to navigating a labyrinth filled with the most intricate and whimsical obstacles imaginable. Here, every decision, from the majestic to the minute, carries the weight of an epic adventure. You are the hero in a saga, where choosing between shades of white can feel as critical as negotiating world peace.

Envision yourself as a masterful conductor, orchestrating a symphony of details ranging from the enchantingly grand to the delightfully mundane. Your journey traverses a landscape dotted with decisions that dance between the magical extremes of an 'enchanted forest' elegance and the cozy charm of your favourite local haunt. In this world, fashioning a dress code becomes an exercise in storytelling, blending narratives of 'fairy tale elegance' with the playful defiance of 'beachside casual.'

But fear not, intrepid planner! The Union Bliss Wedding Planner sails in as your trusted compass, transforming the daunting waves of wedding organization into a voyage of discovery and joy. Imagine having a beacon of calm and clarity, guiding you through storms of decisions and negotiations, ensuring that your journey not only leads to your dream wedding but is also filled with moments of genuine enjoyment and creativity.

With the Union Bliss Wedding Planner in hand, picture yourself weaving through the tapestry of wedding planning with elegance and ease. It is more than a guide; it is your ally in carving out a path that reflects your unique love story, offering you the freedom to explore and express your deepest desires for your special day. Within its pages lie the keys to staying organized, unlocking savings, and, above all, infusing fun into every step towards creating the wedding of your dreams.

This planner is not just about adhering to traditions; it is about tailoring your journey to suit your personal narrative, providing a versatile framework that supports your vision. Whether it is managing guest lists with grace or balancing the budget with creativity, the planner empowers you to master the art of wedding planning.

So, arm yourself with the Union Bliss Wedding Planner and a dash of whimsy, for in the grand celebration of love and commitment, a light-hearted spirit is your most valuable companion. Embrace this planner not merely as a tool, but as a partner in painting your love story onto the canvas of your wedding day. As you turn each page, let the journey enrich you, the choices inspire you, and the anticipation of your perfect day fill you with joy. Before you realize it, you will be stepping into the wedding you have always dreamed of, ready to revel in the masterpiece of memories you have created.

Getting Started

12 MONTHS PRIOR

- ☐ Share the exciting news with a stunning ring pic! Capture the moment and spread the joy.
- ☐ Print this Union Bliss Wedding Planner and create a binder to keep everything organised and in one place.
- ☐ Define your total budget. Plan every detail around this crucial number.
- ☐ Get that engagement sparkler insured. Diamonds are forever, but so is peace of mind.
- ☐ Gather inspiration by exploring Pinterest, wedding blogs and magazines.
- ☐ Envision your dream wedding: traditional or informal, big or small, styles and themes.

Your wedding's visual identity starts with the palette you choose. Dive into the world of colours let your imagination soar and create a wedding that reflects the vibrant tapestry of your love story.

- ☐ Design a Vision Board. Compile a visual representation of your dream wedding. Include your colour palettes, styles and themes.
- ☐ Start looking at ceremony and reception locations.
- ☐ Select a date for your wedding.
- ☐ Throw an engagement party to celebrate and to share the joy with your loved ones.
- ☐ Start putting together a guest list with input from both families. Get a general idea of the size of your wedding.

SHOULD WE INVITE THEM?

Embarking on the journey to decide who gets a golden ticket to your wedding is no small feat. It is a delicate dance of harmonising personal desires, family traditions, and the stark realities of budgeting. This intricate process is truly about striking the perfect chord that resonates with the symphony of your special day. It is a path filled with decisions both tough and tender, but at its core, it is about curating an experience that will echo in your memories for a lifetime.

Here is a blueprint to guide you through the maze of making your wedding guest list, especially when the list is longer than your budget or venue capacity.

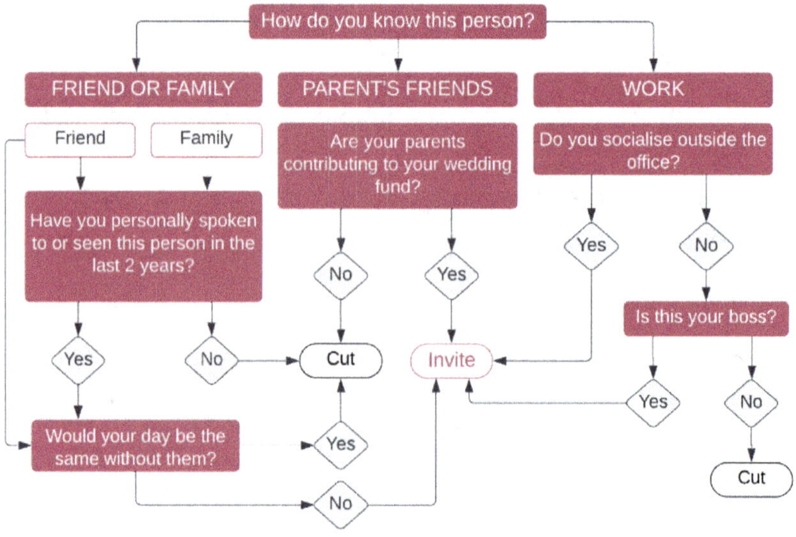

- [ ] Consider a Wedding Planner/Coordinator. Decide if you need professional help (with all your wedding planning or for just on the day coordination) and make the appointment.

- [ ] Make a shortlist of ceremony and reception venues. Schedule up a meeting (take your Wedding Planner/Coordinator with you) to discuss available dates and wedding packages.

IS A WEDDING PLANNER RIGHT FOR YOU?

The journey to your wedding day is paved with decisions, each as crucial as the next in shaping the celebration of your dreams. Among these, deciding whether to hire a wedding planner is a pivotal choice that can influence the flow and feel of your big day. But what exactly does a wedding planner bring to the table, and are they worth the investment? Let us unfold the layers to help you make an informed decision.

♥ THE ROLE OF A WEDDING PLANNER

Imagine having a guardian angel whose sole mission is to bring your wedding vision to life. A wedding planner is part maestro, part confidant, orchestrating every detail from the grandest to the most minute with precision and care. They are your strategic partner in planning, offering a wealth of expertise, insider knowledge, and a treasure trove of vendor connections. From conceptualising the theme to executing the day flawlessly, they cover all bases, ensuring that your journey to 'I do' is as smooth as it is memorable.

♥ THE VALUE ADDED

Hiring a wedding planner might seem like a luxury, but the value they add extends far beyond convenience. Here is a closer look at the benefits:

- Stress reduction: They shoulder the logistical load, transforming what can be a stressful process into a seamless and enjoyable journey.
- Budget management: With a keen understanding of costs, they help navigate your budget effectively, ensuring you get the most bang for your buck.
- Time saving: They streamline the planning process, saving you countless hours of research and coordination.
- Vendor liaison: Their established relationships with vendors can mean better deals and quality service for you.
- Problem-solving: Equipped to manage any hiccup, they ensure your big day unfolds without a glitch, often anticipating and resolving issues before they even arise.

♥ Weighing the Investment

Yes, a wedding planner does represent a significant line item in your wedding budget. However, when you weigh the investment against the time, stress, and potential savings they can offer, the value becomes clear. They not only work to make your dream wedding a reality but can also be instrumental in keeping your expenses in check through smart planning and industry insights.

♥ Making Your Decision

Consider the complexity of your wedding, your personal planning preferences, and your available time. If you are envisioning a large-scale event or your schedule is already stretched thin, a wedding planner could be invaluable. For those with a knack for organization and a tighter budget, a day-of coordinator might suffice, offering support when it is most critical without the full-service price tag

.

In the end, choosing whether to hire a wedding planner is a deeply personal decision that hinges on your unique needs, vision, and circumstances. If peace of mind, expert guidance, and the promise of a beautifully executed wedding day are what you seek, then a wedding planner might just be the key to unlocking the wedding of your dreams.

A WEDDING PLANNER
RIGHT FOR YOU?

YOUR WEDDING *Vision Board*

After the post-engagement butterflies have settled and reality sets in, it is time to embark on the journey of planning your wedding. It is like painting a masterpiece where every brushstroke is a choice that reflects your love story. You will need to determine your wedding preferences, including season, size, style and setting.

Creating a wedding vision board could help you to figure out exactly what you do and do not like and to complete your worksheet. It is the best way to an overall picture of your ideas before you start picking out flowers, attire or even a venue – and to prevent yourself from getting overwhelmed by too many choices. Your wedding vision board (also known as a wedding mood board) will help you organise all your thoughts and ideas in one place, which your vendors will thank you for down the road.

1. CHOOSE YOUR CANVAS

Decide if you want to use a physical or a digital canvas.
If you enjoy crafts, we love the approach of using a cork board with push pins and thumbtacks to piece all your ideas together and move things around if needed.
When it is time to meet vendors, you can bring the board itself or simply snap a few photos. On the other hand, a digital vision board my feel more seamless and easier to share. You can also instantly save ideas that you come across while browsing the internet.

2. COLLECT EVERYTHING THAT INSPIRES YOU

Flip through magazines, bridal catalogues, and other sources to find images, colours, and textures that resonate with your vision. Look for pictures of dresses, flowers, décor, venues, and anything else that inspires you.

♥ THE SCALE OF YOUR CELEBRATION

Extravagant Gala of Love: Envision a grand affair where every moment is a celebration of love, set against a backdrop of opulent grandeur and joyous revelry.

Intimate Elegance: A gathering that strikes the perfect chord between warmth and sophistication, where each guest adds a unique hue to your day.

Cozy Communion: A close-knit celebration where the essence of your love story is shared with every heartfelt exchange, creating memories in an intimate setting.

♥ THE RHYTHM OF YOUR DAY

Choose between the golden hues of a **daytime** wedding, the twinkling stars of a **nighttime** affair, the transitional beauty of an **afternoon-evening** wedding, or the fresh start of a **morning-afternoon** wedding.

♥ THE STAGE FOR YOUR LOVE

Outdoor: Let nature be your witness, under the vast sky or amidst whispering trees.

Indoor: A setting where elegance meets history, with every detail painting a picture of timeless love.

Both: A harmonious blend that moves from the natural grace of the outdoors to the cultivated beauty of an indoor setting.

♥ THE SEASONAL BACKDROP

Whether it is the **Winter**'s Frosty Elegance, **Spring**'s Renewal, **Summer**'s Warm Embrace, or **Autumn**'s Colourful Farewell, each season casts its own magic on your day.

♥ THE HEART OF YOUR CELEBRATION

From art galleries to beaches, castles to vineyards, and everything in between, your **venue** is the cornerstone that supports the vision of your day.

♥ The essence of you

Whether you lean towards bohemian freedom, elegant classicism, modern minimalism, or any **style** that captures your essence, let your wedding reflect the unique blend of personalities that you and your partner bring together.

♥ The Threads of continuity

Your vows can be **traditional, self-written,** or supplemented with **special readings**. Remember, this is your moment to express the depth of your commitment in your own words.

♥ The Soundtrack of Your Love

Choose between a personally curated **playlist**, the dynamic energy of a **DJ**, or the authentic touch of **live musicians/band** to set the tone for your celebration.

♥ The Taste of Joy

From champagne toasts to open bars, and buffet style meals to gourmet full-service dinners, curate a **menu** that delights.

♥ Tokens of Gratitude

Show appreciation with DIY gifts, edible treats, charitable donations, or personalized keepsakes. **Favours** that reflect your shared values.

♥ The Spirit of Celebration

If you feel additional **entertainment** is required, keep the spirits high with a dance party, photobooth fun, karaoke sessions, or engaging games to ensure a memorable experience for all.

♥ The Journey Together

From limousines for grand exits to ensuring comfortable accommodations for you and your guests, every **travel** detail adds to the seamless flow of your wedding festivities.

♥ Extending the Celebration

Whether it is a rehearsal dinner to kick things off, a day-after brunch to wind down, or any other event, these are the moments that **enrich the wedding experience**.

As you sketch out your wedding day, remember that each choice is a stroke of paint on the canvas of your love story. Let your heart and joy guide each decision, crafting a day that is as unique and beautiful as the love you share.

3. Look for a common theme!

Once you have added a few ideas to your wedding vision board, take a step back and try to pick out the recurring elements. Is there a specific colour that keeps showing up? Or a certain type of flower or decor detail that you have saved repeatedly? Look closely for patterns, similarities and an overarching theme throughout your ideas. You might be surprised by what you find.

After you have pulled your ideas together, you can start looking for wedding vendors to bring your vision board to life.

The Next Step

9-12 MONTHS PRIOR

- ☐ Research and book rehearsal dinner, ceremony, and reception venues in your desired location, on your desired date.

- ☐ Begin by selecting your wedding party with care, making them feel special with heartfelt "Will you be my..." cards and a thoughtful small gift.

- ☐ Start the search for the perfect wedding dress, the gown that will make you feel like the radiant star of your love story.

- ☐ Start thinking about bridesmaids and flower girl dresses, ensuring they complement your bridal elegance.

- ☐ The symphony of your special day needs the perfect soundtrack, so consider booking musicians or a DJ for both the ceremony and reception.

- ☐ If your chosen venue does not offer catering services, embark on the culinary journey by booking a caterer who can turn your wedding feast dreams into reality.

- ☐ Capture the magic of your day with a photographer and/or videographer. These professionals will freeze in time the moments that will become the cherished memories of your lifelong journey together.

- ☐ A ceremony without an officiant is like a story without a narrator. Interview and select an officiant who resonates with the spirit of your union.

- ☐ Embrace the charm of your engagement with a photoshoot that captures the essence of your love.

- ☐ As the wedding plans unfold, keep the excitement alive by delving into thoughts of your honeymoon. Dream about the destination that will be the perfect backdrop for the first moments of your married life.

ASSEMBLING YOUR I-DO CREW:
A GUIDE TO PICKING YOUR PARTY PEEPS

Gather round, you starry-eyed lovers! It's time to choose the superhero squad for your love saga—the wedding party. Think of it as drafting your dream team for the ultimate love match, where every player has a pivotal role, from carrying rings to warding off wedding crashers. Let's dive into the who's who of your wedding entourage, shall we?

♥ THE FINE ART OF PICKING YOUR PARTY

Choosing your wedding party is like casting for a blockbuster rom-com: you need stars that shine in their roles and support that keeps the plot moving. Opt for reliability over resume; your college roommate who can't keep a plant alive might not be the best choice for safeguarding the rings. Remember, it's about who knows how to lift your spirits with a well-timed joke, not just who looks good in tuxedos and tutus.

♥ STARRING ROLES:

- **Maid of Honor/Best Man:** Think of them as your love-life coaches—ready to pep-talk you through any pre-wedding jitters, tackle the logistics like pros, and deliver a toast that's equal parts tears and laughter.
- **Bridesmaids/Groomsmen:** Your personal hype crew. From DIY decor disasters to dance floor domination, they're there to ensure your wedding vibes stay as high as your love.
- **Flower Child & Ring Bearer:** Miniature scene-stealers tasked with petal distribution and ring security. Low in height, high in cuteness factor.
- **The Understudies (Junior Bridesmaids/Groomsmen):** Not quite ready for the big leagues, but too talented to keep in the wings. They bring youthful energy and are excellent at bearing signs or giving out programs.

♥ CASTING CALL TIPS:

- **Audition with Care:** Choose people who bring out the best in you, can handle a bit of stress without going full diva, and are willing to dance in ugly shoes if required.
- **Roles for Every Talent:** Not everyone needs to be front and centre. Consider off-stage but crucial roles for your loved ones who shun the spotlight.
- **A Happy Ensemble:** Mix and match personalities wisely. Think of your wedding party as a band—everyone should be in tune, even if they're playing different instruments.

Your wedding party is the supporting cast in your love story's premiere. Choose those who love you, laugh with you, and are ready to embark on this crazy, wonderful journey by your side. After all, they're not just there to look pretty and pose; they're the heart and soul of your celebration, ready to tackle whatever comes your way—from rogue pigeons to misplaced vows—with grace, humour, and perhaps a little bit of mischief.

Securing the dream

6-8 MONTHS PRIOR

- ☐ Secure Your Stunning Gown. The wedding dress that perfectly mirrors your style.

- ☐ Dress Your Besties in Style. Elevate your bridal party by ordering dresses that complement your theme and make your bridesmaids shine.

- ☐ Nail down your guest list, ensuring every cherished individual is accounted for in your celebration of love.

- ☐ Gather those all-important mailing addresses to ensure your invitations reach every corner of your guest list.

- ☐ Spread the love with save-the-dates, sent out six months in advance for local festivities and eight months for destination soirées.

Sending out save the dates and wedding invitations digitally can be a fantastic idea, and it has become increasingly popular in the digital age.

- ♥ Digital invitations are often more budget-friendly than traditional paper invitations. You can save on printing, postage, and other associated costs.

- ♥ Going digital is a greener choice too as it reduces the need for paper and the carbon footprint associated with printing and shipping.

- ♥ Digital invitations are delivered instantly, eliminating postal delays. This is especially useful for last-minute changes or if you have guests from various parts of the world.

- ♥ Digital invitations allow you to include interactive elements such as links to your wedding website, RSVP forms, and even multimedia content like videos or photo galleries.

♥ With digital invitations, you can easily track RSVPs, making it simpler to manage your guest list and plan accordingly.

♥ Digital invitations provide flexibility for updates and changes. If there are any adjustments to the schedule or venue, you can quickly inform your guests through digital communication.

However, it is essential to consider the preferences of your guest list. While many people appreciate the convenience of digital invitations, some may still prefer the traditional feel of a physical invitation. One compromise could be sending digital save the dates and following up with printed wedding invitations. This way, you can enjoy the benefits of both worlds while accommodating your guests' preferences.

- ☐ Seal the deal with your florist or take the DIY route by selecting a flower vendor that resonates with your floral fantasies.
- ☐ Sweeten the deal and indulge your taste buds by choosing the perfect cake with the Cake Connoisseur or caterer of your choice.
- ☐ Soar into wedded bliss by booking your dream accommodation and flights for a honeymoon you will cherish forever.
- ☐ Ensure a warm welcome by reserving accommodations for out-of-town guests, making their stay as delightful as your celebration.
- ☐ Create a charming wedding website to keep your guests in the loop with all the exciting details of your upcoming nuptials.
- ☐ Make it easy for your guests to celebrate your union by creating a registry featuring your favourite picks from select retailers.
- ☐ Finalise the order of your ceremony and deal with the necessary legal documents with your officiant, ensuring a seamless and joyous union.
- ☐ If needed, secure site rentals for tables, chairs, sound systems, lighting, and more, ensuring your venue is as spectacular as your perfect wedding day.

Not long now

3-5 MONTHS PRIOR

- ☐ Design and send out your wedding invitations, setting the tone for your special day.

- ☐ Secure all your stationery needs, from elegant thank you notes to menus, charming place cards, and more!

- ☐ Snag the perfect attire for the groom, groomsmen, ring bearer, and ushers.

- ☐ Elevate your bridal squad's glam with chic accessories like shoes, headpieces, and jewellery.

- ☐ Do not forget your "Something Old, Something New, Something Borrowed, Something Blue".

In the world of weddings, where traditions are treasured and love is celebrated, the age-old adage "Something Old, Something New, Something Borrowed, Something Blue" continues to weave its enchanting magic through ceremonies across cultures.

- ♥ The first element, "Something Old," symbolises the bride's connection to her past. Brides often incorporate a family heirloom – perhaps a piece of jewellery, a veil, or even the gown worn by a beloved grandmother. It is a nod to the wisdom and enduring love that has been woven into the fabric of her familial history.

- ♥ "Something New" embodies optimism, symbolising the couple's journey into the future and the creation of new memories. Modern brides often choose their wedding gown or accessories to represent this element. With each step down the aisle, the bride embraces the promise of a fresh chapter, full of love, growth, and shared adventures.

- ♥ The concept of "Something Borrowed" invites the bride to borrow an item from a happily married friend or family member, imbuing her own union with the positive energy of enduring love. Whether it is a pair of earrings, a veil, or a decorative accessory, this borrowed token serves as a reminder of the support and wisdom shared by those who have walked the path of matrimony before.

♥ The final touch, "Something Blue," has roots in ancient customs that associate the colour blue with fidelity, love, and purity. Brides get creative with this element, incorporating blue flowers, jewellery, or even a discreet blue ribbon on the garter. This subtle splash of colour adds a whimsical and meaningful dimension to the bride's ensemble, signifying the depth of commitment and trust in the union.

In a world that evolves rapidly, these timeless symbols contribute to the rich narrative of the wedding day; reflecting on the couple's deep respect for the past, their excitement for the future, the strength of their support network and the enduring serenity that love brings to their union.

- ☐ Cruise into your wedding day with flair by arranging transportation and booking a hair and makeup trial.

- ☐ Ensure all necessary legal documents for the marriage license and honeymoon are in order.

- ☐ Finalise a delectable menu and beverage selection with your caterer.

- ☐ Order the timeless symbols of love – your wedding bands.

- ☐ Revel in pre-wedding pampering by scheduling beauty appointments for hair, makeup, nails, spa, and tanning for the ultimate glow.

- ☐ Delight your guests with thoughtful favours that reflect your style and gratitude.

- ☐ Choreograph your reception's flow – toasts, speeches, first dance, bouquet toss, cake cutting, and the grand getaway.

- ☐ Ensure your pre-wedding celebrations are a hit by sharing the guest list with hosts of your bridal shower, bachelor, and bachelorette parties, ensuring a celebration to remember.

Just around the corner

2 MONTHS PRIOR

- ☐ Stay on top of RSVPs by keeping your guest list updated.
- ☐ Schedule a meeting with your photographer and videographer to brainstorm stunning shots that capture your special day.
- ☐ Do not forget the details – double-check all bookings with your venues and vendors to ensure a seamless celebration.
- ☐ Share your love story with the community by reaching out to your local newspaper for a wedding announcement.
- ☐ Embrace the joy of your upcoming nuptials with a fabulous bridal shower.
- ☐ Bloom with confidence by confirming flower details with your florist, ensuring your dream blooms will be ready for the big day.
- ☐ Show your appreciation with thoughtful gifts for your wedding party, groom, and parents as a heartfelt thank-you for their support.
- ☐ Cross off important to-dos by securing your marriage license and attending your final dress fitting.
- ☐ Personalise your ceremony by writing heartfelt vows and practicing saying them aloud.
- ☐ Add an individualized touch to your wedding day with printed signage and ensure every detail is picture-perfect.
- ☐ Bring the final touches together by confirming RSVPs from all your guests and reaching out to those you have not heard from yet.
- ☐ Dive into the details with your seating plan and order those charming place cards.

The final countdown

1 MONTH PRIOR

- ☐ Update your caterer with the final guest count and any special meal preferences.

- ☐ Pick-up that gorgeous wedding dress and bridesmaid dresses – do not forget to strut around a bit to break in those fabulous shoes!

- ☐ Pick-up your wedding rings, make sure they sparkle, shine and fit right.

- ☐ Ensure a flawless celebration by confirming delivery details for the cake, flowers and rentals.

- ☐ Have final meetings with your officiant, photographer and videographer before the grand day.

- ☐ Do not forget to pack a wedding-day emergency kit!

- ☐ Seal the deal on your dream honeymoon by confirming all bookings.

- ☐ Let the good times roll with unforgettable bachelor and bachelorette parties.

- ☐ Write heartfelt toasts for both the rehearsal dinner and wedding reception.

- ☐ Delegate like a pro and assign wedding week and day-of responsibilities to your awesome wedding party, such as handing out boutonnières, tipping vendors, clean up, transportation of gifts, returning rentals, etc.

WEDDING DAY EMERGENCY KIT

Things tend to pop up on the wedding day, so it is important that you have a stocked emergency kit in case of accidents, spills or other mishaps.

This is just a few things you can pack into your wedding-day survival kit:

- ♥ *Water*
- ♥ *Tissues*
- ♥ *Antibacterial gel*
- ♥ *Stain remover wipes*
- ♥ *Mini sewing kit*
- ♥ *Band-aids*
- ♥ *Deodorant*
- ♥ *Bug spray*
- ♥ *Drinking straws*
- ♥ *Breath mints*
- ♥ *Bobby pins*
- ♥ *Vitamin C packets*
- ♥ *Lint roller*
- ♥ *Safety pins*
- ♥ *Lip balm*
- ♥ *Body lotion*
- ♥ *Hairspray*
- ♥ *Healthy snacks*
- ♥ *Face wipes*
- ♥ *Clear nail polish*
- ♥ *Pain reliever*
- ♥ *Antacid tablets*
- ♥ *Pen and paper*
- ♥ *Umbrellas*

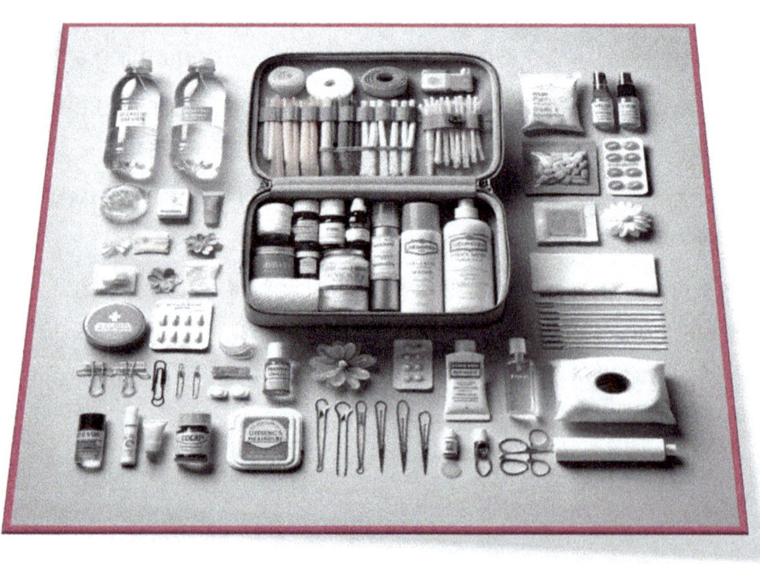

Moments before Forever

WEDDING WEEK

- ☐ Crafting the perfect day requires careful planning and attention to detail. Start by jotting down the day-of timeline and share it with your photographer, videographer, caterer, and any helping hands to ensure everyone is on the same page.

- ☐ Pack your bags for your honeymoon and share your itinerary with close family members just in case of any unforeseen emergencies.

- ☐ Bring the magic to your reception venue by delivering decorations, favours, place cards, the guest book, pens, and any other special items. Make the space uniquely yours.

- ☐ Before the big day, gather your wedding party for a rehearsal, followed by a delightful rehearsal dinner. It is the perfect opportunity to iron out any last-minute details and enjoy some quality time with your closest friends and family.

- ☐ Extend a warm welcome to your any accommodation guests by preparing thoughtful welcome bags and notes. Small gestures can make a big impact.

- ☐ Indulge in some pre-wedding pampering with a relaxing manicure and pedicure, ensuring your hands and feet are ready for the spotlight.

- ☐ Treat yourself to a soothing massage to ease any pre-wedding jitters and ensure you are feeling your absolute best.

- ☐ Lastly, savour the anticipation of the day ahead by striving for a full night of restful sleep. A well-rested bride is a radiant bride.

It has all been worth it!

WEDDING DAY

- [ ] Get ready for the most magical day of your life!
- [ ] Look at the latest weather forecast to ensure smooth sailing on your special day.
- [ ] Throw your overnight bag and honeymoon essentials into the car for an unforgettable journey ahead.
- [ ] Keep your emergency kit within arm's reach – just in case.
- [ ] Share the excitement with your wedding party by handing out day-of timeline to keep everyone on track.
- [ ] Pamper yourself with a fabulous hair and makeup session to feel like the royalty you are.
- [ ] Do not forget to show some love to your amazing bridal squad and groomsmen – surprise them with heartfelt thank-you gifts.
- [ ] With all the planning behind you, it is time to kick back, relax, and soak in every enchanting moment of your wedding day.

THE UNOFFICIAL, YET ABSOLUTELY ESSENTIAL WEDDING DAY ITINERARY

Imagine your wedding ceremony starts at 2 PM; Let us create a wedding day timeline to ensure your big day is as unforgettable (and as stress-free) as finding a parking spot at the mall on Black Friday.

THE MORNING SAGA

♥ 9:00 AM – Rise and Shine! Or hit snooze... just once. It is the big day, after all. Time for breakfast with the crew - think of it as fueling up for the marathon (of joy) ahead.

♥ 9:30 AM – Hair and makeup commence. It is like turning into a superhero, but the cape is your stunning outfit. Groom and pals start primping too. Yes, it takes effort to look this effortlessly charming.

♥ 10:00 AM – Décor and flowers begin their invasion. The venue's transformation is underway, much like your own.

♥ 11:00 AM – Sneaky photo session. Opt for a first look if you want to capture that "You clean up nice!" moment.

THE CALM BEFORE THE STORM

♥ 11:30 AM – Gather the troops. Bridal party and family snapshots. Let us make memories (and pictures you will debate posting on social media).

♥ 1:00 PM – Guests trickle in, finding their seats. Like musical chairs, but everyone wins a seat.

♥ 1:50 PM – Deep breaths. It is almost go-time. Fluff the dress, straighten the tie. Look in the mirror and whisper, "Let's do this."

THE MAIN EVENT

♥ 2:00 PM – Showtime! The ceremony kicks off. Exchange those vows and rings. (Remember, it's "I do," not "I guess so.")

♥ 2:30 PM – Married! Officially. Seal it with a kiss that says, "We survived wedding planning!"

Post-Ceremony Shenanigans

♥ 2:40 PM – More snapshots! Because you can never have too many photos where you look stunningly overjoyed.

♥ 3:00 PM – Cocktail hour: where guests practice the fine art of mingling with a drink in hand. Your cue to vanish for a bit with your new spouse for some "We did it" selfies.

The Feast and Festivities

♥ 4:00 PM – Grand entrance. Think royal wedding meets rock concert. Time to eat, laugh, and be merry.

♥ 4:30 PM – Speeches. Time to find out who's likely to cry first.

♥ 5:00 PM – First dance. Glide across the dance floor (or shuffle awkwardly—it is endearing).

♥ 5:30 PM – Open dance floor. Show off those moves you've been practicing in the living room.

♥ 6:00 PM – Cake cutting. The sweetest arm wrestling match you will ever participate in.

♥ 6:30 PM – Tosses and traditions. Bouquet for the next bride, garter for the next groom, and a dance floor for everyone.

The Grand Finale

♥ 7:30 PM – Last dance. Make it count. No pressure.

♥ 8:00 PM – The big send-off! Like a fairy tale, but with more sparklers and less pumpkin carriage drama.

The Afterparty

♥ 9:00 PM – Vendor exodus. Like Cinderella, they disappear, but leave everything looking like magic happened.

This timeline provides a more relaxed morning and a fuller evening of celebrations. As with any wedding timeline, ensure there's buffer time included for transitions and any unexpected delays.

Coordination with vendors and the venue is crucial to confirm setup times and specific requirements. Consider having a day-of coordinator or a designated person to help keep the day on schedule.

Remember, the best weddings are the ones where you marry your favourite person. Everything else is just icing on the (wedding) cake. Now, go forth and get hitched without a hitch!

Cheers to a day filled with love, laughter, and cherished memories

Navigating post-wedding bliss

HAPPILY EVER AFTER

- [ ] Seal your union with paperwork. Your marriage certificate is more than a document, it is a testament to your love. Essential for name changes and legalities.

- [ ] Your new marital status should reflect in everything from passports to bank accounts. It is the first step in weaving your lives together officially.

- [ ] Harmonize Your Finances (If You Choose). A candid chat about bank accounts and investments can fortify your financial future.

- [ ] Budget for Bliss. Tailor a budget that suits your joint lifestyle, paving the way for a prosperous journey together.

- [ ] Clear those final bills to bid a fond farewell to your vendors.

- [ ] A quick review of all vendor contracts ensures everyone is happy and all terms have been met.

- [ ] Share your experiences with reviews that guide future couples and show gratitude to your vendors.

- [ ] Keep a record of gifts for heartfelt thank-you notes.

- [ ] Personalised notes to your guests are small gestures that leave lasting impressions.

- [ ] Preserve your wedding attire. Treat your dress and suit like the treasures they are.

- [ ] Avoid extra fees by returning borrowed or rented items promptly.

- [ ] Gather your wedding photos and videos to relive the magic.

- [ ] Shout your love from the rooftops and let your professional and social circles know about your new life chapter.

- [ ] Share your happiness with extended friends and family, especially if they could not be there on your special day.

Stress Management

EMBARKING ON A SERENE JOURNEY TO 'I DO'

Planning your wedding is an exhilarating chapter in your love story, yet it is no secret that it can also be a source of stress. However, with the right strategies, you can navigate this journey with grace and joy, ensuring that the path to your special day is as serene as the vows you will exchange. Here are some heartfelt tips to help you manage stress and embrace the beauty of planning your wedding.

♥ BEGIN WITH A BREATH

The key to a stress-free wedding planning experience lies in early preparation. Dive into the details with a clear plan, utilizing tools and apps designed to keep you on track. This early bird approach will ensure you are not caught off guard as your big day approaches.

♥ CRAFT A REALISTIC BUDGET

Your budget is the compass that guides your wedding planning voyage. Setting and adhering to a realistic budget from the start will steer you clear of financial whirlwinds, allowing you to focus on the joy of the occasion.

♥ SHARE THE JOURNEY

Remember, planning your wedding does not have to be a solo flight. Delegate tasks to your partner, family, and friends who are eager to help. This shared experience can deepen bonds, lighten your heart and illuminate your path.

♥ Embrace the Art of Self-Care

Amidst the whirlwind of planning, carve out oases of calm for yourself. Whether it is through yoga, reading, or nature walks, nurturing your well-being is paramount.

♥ Keep Your Eyes on the Horizon

When the details become overwhelming, anchor yourself in the reason behind the celebration—your love story. This perspective is a powerful antidote to stress.

♥ Simplify

While DIY projects can add a personal touch, they can also lead to burnout. Be judicious in your DIY endeavours, focusing on what truly brings you joy without overextending yourself.

♥ Communicate and Compromise

Your wedding is a reflection of your joint journey. Regularly sharing your thoughts and feelings with your partner can fortify your bond and distribute the emotional load.

♥ Establish Boundaries

It is natural for family and friends to offer advice, but it is also okay to kindly assert your wishes. Setting clear boundaries can prevent external pressures from clouding your vision.

♥ Pause and Reflect

Intentionally setting aside days to step away from wedding planning can recharge your spirit and renew your enthusiasm for the journey ahead.

♥ CONSIDER A GUIDING HAND

If your budget allows, a wedding planner can be a beacon of peace, expertly navigating the complexities of planning, allowing you to savour the anticipation of your wedding day.

♥ CULTIVATE INNER PEACE

Integrating mindfulness into your daily routine can anchor you in the present, transforming stress into tranquillity.

♥ PRIORITIZE HEALTH

A balanced diet, regular physical activity, and sufficient sleep are the pillars of stress management, nurturing both mind and body as you plan your wedding.

♥ EMBRACE FLEXIBILITY

Having a Plan B for potential hitches can provide peace of mind, knowing that come what may, your day will be beautiful.

Remember,

the essence of your wedding lies in the celebration of love, not in the perfection of every detail. By embracing these strategies, you can weave a tapestry of joy and serenity as you step toward your future together, stress-free.

Setting the budget

Embarking on the journey toward your dream wedding is an enthralling adventure, blending the excitement of bringing your vision to life with the critical task of making decisions that mirror your unique love story. Recognizing the importance of navigating these decisions with a keen eye on finances, we have meticulously crafted a bespoke tool tailored for the DIY couple. Our comprehensive table serves as an essential resource for meticulously tracking every facet of your celebration, from the choice of venue to the delicate nuances of decor. This table transcends its function as a mere planning tool; it acts as your navigational compass through the complex terrain of wedding planning, empowering you to make informed, budget-conscious decisions without sacrificing your vision.

Picture the process of crafting your wedding budget as painting a masterpiece, where each stroke and colour choice contributes to the emergence of a breathtaking tableau. Approximately 40-50% of your canvas—your budget—is devoted to the grandeur of your venue, the gastronomic delights, and the essential rentals that lay the foundation for your celebration. A further 10-12% is dedicated to immortalizing these moments through the lenses of adept photographers and videographers. Another 8-10% is allocated for attire and beauty, ensuring you and your partner radiate on your special day, with an equal portion reserved for florals and decor that infuse life and vibrancy into every corner.

Music and laughter, the soul of your celebration, command 7-8% of your budget, setting the tone for an unforgettable experience. Invitations and stationery, the bearers of your love story, warrant 2-3%, while a contingency reserve of 5-10% safeguards against any unforeseen expenses, preserving the integrity of your meticulously crafted plan.

To bring this conceptual framework to life, we present a pie chart that delineates the recommended wedding budget allocation. As illustrated, the lion's share is devoted to the venue, catering, and rentals, underscoring the pivotal role these components play in sculpting the overall wedding experience. Each segment of the pie chart corresponds to a distinct category of wedding expenses, facilitating a visual comprehension of how to judiciously distribute your budget. This chart is not prescriptive but rather a foundational guide, inviting you to customize the allocations in alignment with your personal values and the unique contours of your wedding.

The dimensions of your guest list, the venue's locale, the timing of your celebration, and the aspects you wish to accentuate all influence your budgetary blueprint. If your wedding is a collaborative endeavour, incorporating contributions from family, it transforms into a rich mosaic of shared aspirations and resources, marking not merely a day, but the inauguration of your collective journey.

Let this guide embolden you to approach your wedding planning with creativity and confidence, utilizing your budget as the bedrock for a day that not only aligns with but elevates your unique love story. With strategic planning and our indispensable table at your disposal, your wedding is poised to exceed your loftiest dreams, heralding the start of your marital voyage in the most memorable and personalized manner.

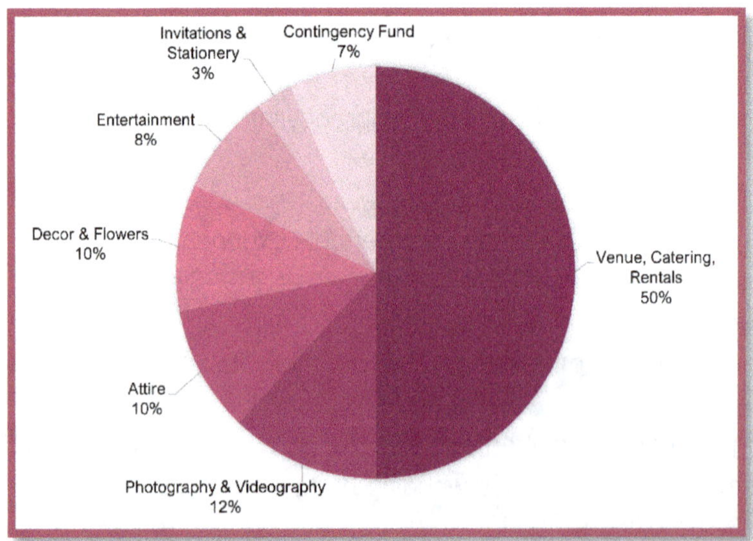

Wedding Budget

TOTAL WEDDING BUDGET:

Bride's family: _______________   Groom's family: _______________   Groom & Bride: _______________

CEREMONY AND RECEPTION				
ITEM	COST/ESTIMATE	ACTUAL SPEND	VARIANCE	NOTES
Wedding Planner / Coordinator				
Reception Venue Location Fee				
Reception Venue Rentals				
Reception Music				
Ceremony Location Fee				
Photobooth				
Ceremony Musicians / Music				

CEREMONY AND RECEPTION

ITEM	COST/ESTIMATE	ACTUAL SPEND	VARIANCE	NOTES
Catering				
Bar service fee				
Bartenders				
Cake(s) and Cutting Fee				
Rehearsal Dinner Venue				
Officiant Fee/Donation				
Transportation				
Parking				
Ring pillow / box				
Flower girl basket				
Guest Book				
Wedding Night Accommodation				
SUBTOTAL				

FLOWERS AND DÉCOR

ITEM	COST/ESTIMATE	ACTUAL SPEND	VARIANCE	NOTES
Bride's Bouquet				
Bridesmaid's bouquets				
Throw-away bouquet				
Flower girl's flowers				
Altarpiece				
Reception Decorations				
Ceremony Decorations				
Other ceremony flowers				
Corsages				
Boutonnieres				
Reception Centrepieces				
Tip Money for Vendors				
SUBTOTAL				

PHOTO AND VIDEO

ITEM	COST/ESTIMATE	ACTUAL SPEND	VARIANCE	NOTES
Engagement shoot				
Photographer				
Wedding album				
Parent's albums				
Additional prints				
Videographer				
SUBTOTAL				

STATIONERY

ITEM	COST/ESTIMATE	ACTUAL SPEND	VARIANCE	NOTES
Save-the-Dates				
Invitations and reply-cards				
Programmes				

STATIONERY

ITEM	COST/ESTIMATE	ACTUAL SPEND	VARIANCE	NOTES
Place cards				
Menus				
Seating chart				
Thank-you cards				
Other signage				
Postage				
Rehearsal Dinner Invitations				
SUBTOTAL				

GIFTS

ITEM	COST/ESTIMATE	ACTUAL SPEND	VARIANCE	NOTES
For each other				
Guest's favours				
Maid of honour				

GIFTS

ITEM	COST/ESTIMATE	ACTUAL SPEND	VARIANCE	NOTES
Bridesmaids				
Best man				
Groomsmen				
Parents of the bride				
Parents of the groom				
Readers / other participants				
Welcome gifts				
GIFTS: SUBTOTAL				

ATTIRE

ITEM	COST/ESTIMATE	ACTUAL SPEND	VARIANCE	NOTES
Wedding dress				
Headpiece and veil				
Bridal shoes				

ATTIRE

ITEM	COST/ESTIMATE	ACTUAL SPEND	VARIANCE	NOTES
Lingerie / hosiery / Garter				
Jewellery and accessories				
Hair appointments				
Make-up appointments				
Dress preservation				
Beauty appointments				
Wedding rings				
Groom's tuxedo or suit				
Groom's shoes				
Groom's accessories				
Groom's cufflinks / lapel pin				
Outfit for ring bearer and usher(s)				
Bridesmaid's dresses				
Bridesmaid's shoes				

ATTIRE

ITEM	COST/ESTIMATE	ACTUAL SPEND	VARIANCE	NOTES
Bridesmaid's accessories				
Dress(es) for flower girl(s)				
Honeymoon clothes				
SUBTOTAL				

OTHER EVENTS

ITEM	COST/ESTIMATE	ACTUAL SPEND	VARIANCE	NOTES
Engagement party				
Bridal shower				
Bachelorette party				
Bachelor party				
Rehearsal dinner				
SUBTOTAL				

HONEYMOON

ITEM	COST/ESTIMATE	ACTUAL SPEND	VARIANCE	NOTES
Airfares				
Transportation				
Activities				
Meals and drinks				
Shopping				
Passport and visa				
Vaccinations and medications				
Luggage				
Clothing				
Personal care				
SUBTOTAL				

OTHER

ITEM	COST/ESTIMATE	ACTUAL SPEND	VARIANCE	NOTES
Unexpected costs				
OTHER: SUBTOTAL				

Wedding Purchases

DATE	ITEM	ACTUAL COST	DEPOSIT PAID	BALANCE DUE	DATE DUE	PAID
						☐
						☐
						☐
						☐
						☐
						☐
						☐
						☐
						☐
						☐
						☐

DATE	ITEM	ACTUAL COST	DEPOSIT PAID	BALANCE DUE	DATE DUE	PAID
						☐
						☐
						☐
						☐
						☐
						☐
						☐
						☐
						☐
						☐
						☐
						☐
						☐
						☐
						☐

Vendors

In the whirlwind of planning your dream wedding, finding the perfect vendors plays a pivotal role in bringing your vision to life. It is here that our

specially designed vendor worksheets come into play, acting as your personal navigator through the vibrant world of wedding planning. These invaluable tools are more than just lists; they are your roadmap to making choices that resonate with your personal style, budget, and the unique essence of your love story.

Crafted with care, these worksheets offer a detailed comparison of services, prices, and packages, allowing you to weigh your options with clarity and confidence. It is about creating a day that reflects your journey together, a celebration that will remain etched in your hearts forever. With our vendor worksheets, you are not just planning an event; you are crafting an experience that is as seamless as it is memorable.

Imagine the joy of planning your wedding, free from the stress of uncertainty, with every choice a step closer to the celebration you have always dreamed of. This guide is your ally, transforming the daunting into the doable, and turning your wedding planning journey into an adventure filled with excitement and anticipation. Let us embark on this journey together, making every moment count towards the day when your dreams become reality.

WEDDING PLANNER / COORDINATOR

Name:

Phone:

Email:

Website:

Address:

Payment policy:

Cancellation policy:

ITEM	BUDGET	COST / ESTIMATE	SPENT
TOTAL:			

NOTES

WEDDING VENUE

Venue name:

Contact:

Phone: Email:

Wedding date:

Venue opening time: Venue closing time:

Address:

Payment policy:

Cancellation policy:

ITEM	BUDGET	COST / ESTIMATE	SPENT
TOTAL:			

NOTES

PHOTOGRAPHY

Vendor name:

Contact:

Phone: Email:

Address:

Engagement shoot date/time:

Number of photographers:

Photographer hours at wedding:

Options for additional hours:

Will I get digital files:

Date that photos/files will be available:

Back-up plan if photographer is sick:

Payment policy:

Cancellation policy:

ITEM	BUDGET	COST / ESTIMATE	SPENT
TOTAL:			

NOTES

VIDEOGRAPHY

Vendor name:

Contact:

Phone: Email:

Address:

Number of videographers:

Videographer hours at wedding:

Options for additional hours:

Date that video will be available:

Online hosting options:

Back-up plan if videographer is sick:

Payment policy:

Cancellation policy:

ITEM	BUDGET	COST / ESTIMATE	SPENT
TOTAL:			

NOTES

CATERING

Vendor name:

Contact:

Phone: Email:

Menu choice:

Address:

Payment policy:

Cancellation policy:

ITEM	BUDGET	COST / ESTIMATE	SPENT
TOTAL:			

NOTES

DÉCOR RENTAL

Vendor name:

Contact:

Phone: Email:

Address:

Pick-up or delivery time:

Payment policy:

Cancellation policy:

ITEM	BUDGET	COST / ESTIMATE	SPENT
TOTAL:			

NOTES

CAKE

Vendor name:

Contact:

Phone: Email:

Address:

Pick-up or delivery time:

Special request:

Payment policy:

Cancellation policy:

ITEM	BUDGET	COST / ESTIMATE	SPENT
TOTAL:			

NOTES

STATIONERY

Vendor name:

Contact:

Phone: Email:

Address:

Payment policy:

Cancellation policy:

ITEM	BUDGET	COST / ESTIMATE	SPENT
TOTAL:			

NOTES

FLOWERS

Vendor name:

Contact:

Phone: Email:

Address:

Pick-up or delivery time:

Payment policy:

Cancellation policy:

ITEM	BUDGET	COST / ESTIMATE	SPENT
TOTAL:			

NOTES

HAIR

Vendor name:

Contact:

Phone: Email:

Address:

Trial run appointment date/time:

Wedding day appointment date/time:

Payment policy:

Cancellation policy:

ITEM	BUDGET	COST / ESTIMATE	SPENT
TOTAL:			

NOTES

MAKE-UP

Vendor name:

Contact:

Phone: Email:

Address:

Trial run appointment date/time:

Wedding day appointment date/time:

Payment policy:

Cancellation policy:

ITEM	BUDGET	COST / ESTIMATE	SPENT
TOTAL:			

NOTES

FAVOURS

Vendor name:

Contact:

Phone: Email:

Address:

Pick-up or delivery time:

Payment policy:

Cancellation policy:

ITEM	BUDGET	COST / ESTIMATE	SPENT
TOTAL:			

NOTES

TRANSPORTATION

Vendor name:

Contact:

Phone: Email:

Address:

Pick-up time:

Payment policy:

Cancellation policy:

ITEM	BUDGET	COST / ESTIMATE	SPENT
TOTAL:			

NOTES

Guest List

YOUR WEDDING VIP ROSTER

Think of your wedding guest list as the ultimate VIP roster for the party of a lifetime. It is not just a list of names; it is a carefully curated collection of stars in the blockbuster event of your year. From Aunt Edna with her five cats to your college roommate who still owes you for pizza, each name brings its own flavour to the mix. Jotting down addresses, RSVPs, chicken-or-fish preferences, and those quirky notes about who needs a booster seat or a dance floor free from peanuts is crucial. It is like being the director of your own rom-com, ensuring every scene (or seating arrangement) is picture-perfect and every guest feels like a celeb.

Why obsess over this list? Because it is the magical formula that ensures Uncle Bob is far enough from the DJ to keep his hearing aid intact, and your vegan friends have more than just salad to Instagram. It is about avoiding those "oops" moments when you realize you forgot to invite your mom's new beau and ensuring your budget does not blow up like a surprise fireworks finale. In short, your guest list is the secret sauce to pulling off a celebration that is as smooth as your fiancé's dance moves are not. So, grab that pen, channel your inner event planner, and let us make this guest list one for the history books—or at least one that does not end up with crashed servers and epic tales of who almost did not make the cut!

EXAMPLE OF A BASIC GUEST LIST ENTRY:

Name(s):

Children:

Address:

Phone: Email:

☐ Save the date sent   # attending:

☐ Invitation sent   Table number:

☐ RSVP received   Gift:

☐ Thank you card sent   Meal choice:

Notes:

Name(s):

Children:

Address:

Phone: Email:

☐ Save the date sent   # attending:

☐ Invitation sent   Table number:

☐ RSVP received   Gift:

☐ Thank you card sent   Meal choice:

Notes:

EXAMPLE OF A DETAILED GUEST LIST ENTRY:

Name(s):

Children:

Address:

Phone: Email:

\# attending: ☐ Pre-wedding event

Table number: ☐ Post-wedding event

☐ Save the date sent   ☐ Engagement party

☐ Invitation sent   ☐ Bridal shower

☐ RSVP received   ☐ Bachelor party

☐ Thank you card sent   ☐ Bachelorette party

Meal choice: Gift:

Notes:

Name(s):

Children:

Address:

Phone: Email:

\# attending: ☐ Pre-wedding event

Table number: ☐ Post-wedding event

☐ Save the date sent   ☐ Engagement party

☐ Invitation sent   ☐ Bridal shower

☐ RSVP received   ☐ Bachelor party

☐ Thank you card sent   ☐ Bachelorette party

Meal choice: Gift:

Notes:

The final stroke of your wedding masterpiece

In the grand tapestry of your wedding journey, the final chapter is not just about tying loose ends but embracing the unexpected twists and turns with grace and poise. As you navigate through the enchanting labyrinth of wedding planning, remember that the Union Bliss Wedding Planner serves as your initial compass, guiding you through the myriad of choices and challenges with wisdom and wit. Yet, beyond its pages, lies the vast expanse of your creativity and resourcefulness, a realm where an endless supply of lists and information awaits your command.

In the alchemy of your imagination, you are free to conjure additional lists, gather bespoke advice, and curate a trove of resources that resonate with your personal tale of love and commitment. This planner sets the stage, offering the essential scaffolding upon which you can build, embellish, and refine your vision to as close to perfection as the whims of fate allow.

Embrace this journey with the knowledge that while the Union Bliss Wedding Planner illuminates the path, your journey is infinitely yours to shape. It is in the interplay of preparation and spontaneity, the dance between the planner's guidance and your own innovative spirit, that your wedding day will unfold as a masterpiece of memories, a celebration imbued with your essence and elevated by the unexpected.

So, as you stand on the brink of this once-in-a-lifetime voyage, let the Union Bliss Wedding Planner be your guide, your foundation. Yet, dare to dream, to innovate, and to chart your own course. In the end, it is your heart, your vision, and your endless creativity that will craft the wedding of your dreams, a day as unique and unforgettable as your love story itself.

Get in touch

If you're embarking on the exciting journey of wedding planning and find yourself in need of further information or guidance, we invite you to reach out to us. The 'Union Bliss Wedding Planner' team is dedicated to assisting you in making your wedding day as perfect and seamless as possible. Whether you have questions about the guidebook, need advice on navigating the planning process, or seek personalized support, we're here to help. Contact us via email at info@unionbliss.co.za or explore our website at www.unionbliss.co.za for additional resources. Let us be a part of making your dream wedding a reality.